More for Helen of Troy

Also by Simon Mundy

Poetry
Letter to Carolina
By Fax to Alice Springs
After the Games

More for Helen of Troy

Simon Mundy

SEREN

Seren is the book imprint of
Poetry Wales Press Ltd.
57 Nolton Street, Bridgend, Wales, CF31 3AE
www.serenbooks.com

The right of Simon Mundy to be identified as
the author of this work has been asserted in accordance
with the Copyright, Designs and Patents Act, 1988.

© Simon Mundy 2012

ISBN: 978-1-85411-578-2

A CIP record for this title is available from the British Library.

The publisher acknowledges the financial assistance of the Welsh Books Council.

Cover art: Photograph 'Deceptive Beauty' © Ewgeniya Lyras
www.ewgeniyalyras.com

Printed in Bembo by Berforts Group, Stevenage.

Contents

III

Hair Day

The braiding could take a morning
From dawn, when the other women
Yawned, too stiff to flaunt their lesser virtues,
Through the brilliance of the southern sun,
Its brightening echoed in the lightening
Of her strands from reddish gold to almost white.
Only far below, the place of Paris,
Did a dark shadow expose the soul,
Even that mown and ordered
To obedient falsehood.

IV

Deceptive Beauty

She carries all the contradictions
Of peonies, body and soul,
Bloom and stem, held proud in Spring,
First and fast to rise. Her face a glory

Budding in a perfect moon, a mystery
So contained, complex in hidden folds,
So fecund in astonishing conclusion.
In full June panoply she seems

Gaspingly beautiful, her white cheeks
Tinged with pink, her neck flecked
With clever hints of colour, her scent
Pervasive late into the cathartic evening.

Her petal skin, though, flinches
At the slightest touch, bruises even
From a kiss of admiration,
Collapses as soon as picked,

A sigh of quick capitulation.
Your sadness is misplaced, don't worry,
For though she hates to be moved
Her roots will be among the earliest

To sense the death of frost,
Pierce the reluctant earth
And send her incarnation
Shooting from her bed again.

V

Parade

She rarely shows herself in person,
Reachable flesh, febrile scent,
Cause enough for a riot, another assault,
Escalating her protective walls, tearing aside
Her screen of indifference. But her image
Is everywhere – icon and full-length,
Embellished and crude, accurate and all make-up.

Sometimes, before the men go out to fight,
To line up for destruction, they parade
Everything they've got of her, portraits
So ideal they take the breath away and leave
Their bearers reckless for castigation.

VI

Menelaus's Song

All that has gone is time
Elastic hours and nights at sea,
Around the fires fuelled with sticks
The goats left and the skeletons
Of passing ships. I tried to see you
As you were the night before our parting,
Those hours of astonishment, discovery and fear
So fleet beside these barren years.

All I can summon is the icon,
The flat ideal of beauty
Seen through another's eye
And I dread the reuniting minutes,
You torn from your ruptured city
Wearing the lines and paint of exile
The resignation of a trophy handed back.

VII

Paris' Song

You are a judge of course
As well as supplicant and victim,
So what will my sentence be?
A napier to your household,
Counting the cost, laundering,
Rinsing the unfortunate past
From your bright future
And all the distressing while
Acting as banker to your dreams.

VIII

The Soldier's Song

She is so far away
I have never smelled her skin,
Felt the texture of her dress,

Once a voice sounded silken enough to fit
The official picture but it was nothing
I could prove – just a distant
Parting of the air that carried hope.

No woman I have touched is worth my life
No goddess needs it
But she is not for touching
And the years will leave her
Warm when I am mud.

IX

Menelaus Reports

That first night together again
When all that had happened in between
Came down on our tongues like kitchen weights,
We couldn't decide where to put our hands,
Whether to flutter them, trapped birds of apology,
Or hold, trace a line of memory.

How could you be the same?
Life's wars produce their little changes,
Damp patches on your fresco,

So desire was not the old desire,
Fraught with possession, pushed
To the limits of your acceptance,
But the slow joy of visiting
A half-remembered clearing in the woods
And finding wild strawberries
Growing there, beneath a fallen oak
Just as they always did.

X

Valediction

There have been and will be
Many powerful queens and women
Who drive boys to war,
Girls of every land will suffer
The terrors of your life,
The intrusion of strangers
Deep in the guts, the abiding hurt
No kindness can assuage,
But none will claim such beauty
That the gods become
As bellicose as men.

Mermaid

This rock, this divan of stone
Is too jagged for your tail, tearing
Young scales, the salt of sea and tears
Searing raw skin as you preen and comb,
Holding the pose for shipsful of men
Who pass in the morning.
What else can you do?
Hide in the cold northern waters that sparkle
On the surface but hold poisons that pock
Your fins with dirty sores.
Or you could hitch on board those ships,
Shed the tail, rejoice in legs and bush,
Bask on the warm sands of love
Before the mortal tides creep in
Across the disappointing strand.
No. Keep amphibious. Immortal
Beauty is worth a little weeping.

An Incident of War

Beyond midnight curfewed hands sought sanctuary
In the crypts of bodies primed for implosion.
The car rocked, imitating the breath of the distant sea
In obedience to the moonlight over the street,
Empty save for the free contentment of intent lovers
Caught by the watching sky full of rigid wings.

Besieged families had been left to the ruins, the fundamentals
Of their bickering, the petty caveats and forbiddings,
The creeds of good behaviour in atrocious times.
Across the world no caress went unnoticed,
No kiss born again without approval;

On this alone the invading and parental tribes agreed.
Such bush fires had to be snuffed out.

Whose was the cry of victory? Whose
Red line finding whose spot? Whose moral
Mountain? Whose transit of Venus?
Whose perpetual dust?

Four Lyrics

I

Water cannot be compressed
But in that uncontrite volume
More elements can lie dissolved
Than in any self-admiring wine.
The surface is shield and invitation
To this high lake beneath the fragile mountain top
(Cracked by erosion but proud summit nonetheless)
Abandoned by its glacier,
Rarely fed but often raided.

II

I kiss to be expelled,
Withdraw to draw the sortie.
It is a feint
For you rest,
Stare out calmly,
A fortified inch from my hand,
Secure in your decision that I will be
Tolerated but never pampered,
Indulged in anger or desire.

III

Impregnable
Like the old forts on tall hills
That defied all the assaults of Italy,
The Imperial ambitions
The promises of comfort and alliance.
Such formidable defences,
Rampart after rampart,
Vicious pointed stakes lining every ditch and gully,
A taunt of arrows, stones and
Fire for the unwanted visitor.
But time is for biding
The stone's throw to the river a mile too far
When the besieger is camped on the bank.
Seldom did the warrior's heart let her believe
The lesson from all the other forts.
That swift surrender was the only certain way
To forestall the sky from falling on her head.

IV

I open to you like flowers straining for the sun.
Swish. There.
Beheaded with one swipe
Barely pausing in your stride
You have rid the garden of me.

Topkapi Cat

When the revolution came,
Eight generations earlier,
Your ancestor said the guards' bright
Costumes dimmed to khaki, girls
Ambled outside the harem,
Mice multiplied and though at night
It became your silent playground
There were no cushions, no fires,
No kitchens, no fallen viziers
Seeking the comfort of a purr,
Warm fur and the sweet lament of the oud.

A Prayer for a New God-daughter

Preserve the moment
When nothing is decided:
Not name, not the pace
Or direction of childhood,
The shape or frequency of love,
The pull of money, home or duty.
Cry for the future and smile
At your new day, the few already past,
And let no-one organise your mind,
Dictate your prayers or their destination.
Let your conquests be in hearts
And your mercy boundless.
Do not blame the silence
If you cannot hear the songs,
For they are all yours to compose.

Afternoon Excuse

It seemed the perfect lie
Nonlucent, impervious, elegant.
So it remained for a day
From the first insistent message
To the fluent second, too fluent,
The embellishment, the doubt trigger
The new unnecessary place where you
Had to be for the satisfaction of the gods.
Did you decide early or only
In the morning when the dread set in?

Society Haiku

So, Mr. Prufrock,
How's the rest of your week look?
Mega exciting?

Translated Daughter

After Auden
and the art of Klara Pokrzywko

Translated daughter
Who prints a foot
Into virgin paper
Or compliant silver
Leaves a torso
To bronze in the sun,
Takes the sweat
Of spent bodies
Tainting the sheets
And hangs them
To dry in the wind.
Come down then
And blend the acid
With immortal fire
To catch a version
Of your arms and teats
Your curling lips
Against this skin
Startle this itinerant
Mortal to perform
And serenade
The natal moment
We transform
This sombre night
Into glorious dawn.

Olympic Love

You are my cauldron, my petals of flame
Consuming hope, dropping molten rings
Here, there, nowhere near enough
For even a pentathlete to reach your body.
I want you to dive from aeroplane high clouds,
Cut the water silently, touch and score gold.
When you step up to bow your head
For the medal, freshly cast, this special anthem
Will banish nations and tell how you,
My sweet youth across the world,
Have gathered at these games for me alone.

The New Senedd, Cardiff

A Poem for the Opening, St. David's Day 2006.

Watch the words fly in their aviary of toughened
Glass, mingling with other languages,
Obfuscating in front of everybody as if it were decent
To debate without resolution, their consonants
Finished with the thud of English,
The crack of Welsh drugging meaning
Until they float from the chimney of the politics bothy
Or are netted, protesting their innocence
And captured digitally for all to read,
Shameless in the cold of history.

A Vote for Absence

That was an unusual manifesto by any standards,
A plea for anti-votes, for noughts not crosses.
The crosses were no protection
And the noughts contained no promises.
Thirteen candidates were enough to cause
Alarm but escape from the conclusions was futile,
The message from the people clear but silent.

All twelve party candidates had voted crossly for themselves,
Thirty-three thousand, three hundred and thirty-seven voters
Approved their choice with nought. Abstentions won.
The others were all equally cancelled, the noughty manifesto
Adopted – no more laws nor regulations,
Three terms results in surfeit, redundancy rules.

Lines...

Commemorating the European Commission Conference 'Dialogue Between Peoples and Cultures: the Artists and Cultural Actors, Held for Two Days in Brussels' Palais de Beaux Arts (BOZAR) During the Brussels Bravo Festival, February 2005 under the Patronage of President Barroso of the Commission and Repeated at the Berliner Konferenz A Soul For Europe, November 2007 to Official Acclaim.

Men spoke and left
A heap of words.
Gradually the molten breath
Set hard,
Syllables married phrases
Helixed into paragraphs.
Soon we had a mountain,
A jagged unloved peak,
The accidental
Inconsequential spoils
Of Europe's thought.

Mohammed will not come
To this mountain
And no-one has the money
To move it.

Citrus

Above Manhattan the clouds were trying to snow
Paltry flakes, apologies
For America's apocalyptic weather.
We had a rendezvous for Amsterdam Avenue
On a Sunday uncomplicated in any way
The Baptists in their funeral house
Or the Jews next door would understand.
Instead you melted away like the fire trucks
After they failed to find a fire,
Like the love of the couple at the adjacent table
As babies were discussed and her
Desire became his discarded theory.
The snow came to nothing and the lemon trees
Stayed green without the bitterness of fruit.

Windows

Looking out from your twin windows
The view changes little with the hours,
A wall, some graffiti, multicoloured,
Left by small men with few words.
You wait for the scene to shift,
For true landscape to be revealed,
Then the brown curtains that shield
The inside, forbid outsiders to peer through,
Will be drawn, letting the sun
Tint the sparkling lenses green,
Granting rare permission to approach
The soul, not yet with understanding
But with a silent clue.

Collusion

Altay and Smokey Mountains,
Siberia and North Carolina

I have slept between these mountains before
And heard the river swirl perpetually
Interrupting dreams and the cries
Of excited children on the rocks.
Another continent, enemy country
Hosted me then, held me
Hostage for the weekend, secured
By ropes of hospitality, expectant smiles.

The mountains curve gently, letting trees
Creep up their skirts all the way
To the summit. Valleys are nursed
Down to the plains, easing the summer heat.

Without the people sharpening their languages
The mountains know they are cousins
Stranded like colonial lovers around the world.
Now and then they remember each other,
Sigh contentedly, and tip settlers
Skirmishing through the rapids.

Radnor Songs

I

The Buzzard

On the ridge above Radnor
Four barrows prick the skyline
Half moons for the bones of kings
Who became pointers to the stars.
Now their hunting fields are mine
For I can out-span their arms
Swoop faster than their rabble,
With a cry soar and open
Their horizon to the falling sun.

II

Four

I've lost the key, no
It's worse than that.
I've lost the lock,
The secret, the reason
For the secret
Four
Always guarded by four
Corners of a circle
Castles in the south
Forts from a time when
Iron meant victory
Not slag and unemployment,
Barrows on the crest
Stones for sun and constellations
Quarters for soldiers.
What for?
All I have
Is a list of what has been,
The feeling of missing
Fun, sport, import, point
All four.

III

Summergill

Sewing the field patchwork idly
Caring nothing for irregular sides,
Making noises that soothe the animals,
Ingratiate the birds and lure
Weekend lovers to your blooming meadows,
You are the perfect gill for summer.
Major brook, non-commissioned river,
Winter roar worth little more
Than a minor flood.
Who now can hear the ice that gave you birth
Or in your feline waters
Taste the warrior blood?

IV

Flat Out

Flat out, stretched with no more to say
After we had made the earth our altar,
Sown, reaped and threshed under the full sun,
We lay, gazed at the buzzard circling
High enough to mistake us for prey.
In this strange field we had been a sacrifice,
Content leeching into the shorn grass
Four millennia after the lost knife
Had caught the glint of a midsummer morning
In the national stadium, cathedral close
Bounded by posts the width of forty year oaks.
You sang, and round the valley
Delighted larks understudied the ghosts.

V

Radnor (New)

What ambitious streets this city has,
Broad enough for oxen, hay and castle stone,
Straight and crossed as a grid for New York
Four centuries too early.
The church would kid you it's Italian
But this is no Verona,
No room for a piazza or even a café,
No colonnades to strut among the plotting ladies,
No opera nor dancing den.
Radnor sighs and wails
For enlightened settlers
With more energy than time.

VI

Radnor (Old), Church and Harp

Caught between the placid green of hopeless farms
And the road rush, fleeing or seeking cities,
Each tree and turf flank shields an era,
The rubbish of violence, the boundaries of lost significance.
A path leads nowhere, ditch to bramble patch,
Pint to table, pub to bungalow
Instead of castle moat to thoroughfare,
Stadium to sanctuary.
There is no truculent Roman, or Conqueror's
Man-at-arms, no rebel or persecuted priest.
The chariots rot beneath unnecessary sheep,
Aristocrats have dismissed their servants,
Sold their mansions to democracy, rabbits breed
Where chieftains sacrificed
For a benign scene such as this
Ravaged by tranquillity.

Presteigne Festival/Gwaithla 25 Years On

Where I planted a slender hedge
A damson forest spreads across the field
And apple, cherry and copper beach
Have shrugged off their sapling support,
Hold their own against the storms with confidence.

The curlews have fled the breeding buzzards
And the faithful swallows have left the bats
Their stretch of roof which sags where the builder
Once said, rightly, it would last for years.
Outside, in front, the ground has risen perceptibly.

A century has changed, a quarter passed,
A generation's beauty has furrowed and eroded,
Desire crumbled into bitter flakes
Through parenthood and worse, our circumference
Grown without accomplishment to match.

Music, once so new it frightened,
Now rests easy in the catalogue of old invention
Waiting for revival, measured by fresh fingers,
Counted, like us, quite sweet, motherly
Though misshapen by neglect and time.

The plans have progressed from paper
To ash, to compost nurturing
The accidental damsons. Will there be
Hours enough, and inclination
And hope to reap their fruit?

The Island

I

The party started at three in the morning, give or take
                                  a hoot and whoop,
Became a near riot as the little road clogged with mokes
And jeeps and rattletrap trucks
Delivering fuck-you boys to the beach
And clever-clever girls to the music by the sea.

Friday night, Friday Fight Night,
When the horns are worn and sounded,
Conch against car, parish against parish.

Only the dawn brings peace to these tidy rioters
Who love and leave nothing broken in the wrack.

II

How did we know the world would never be the same again?

We had seen the rain coming towards us across the sea before,
Though mainly in the morning, out of season, with a wind
                                        basking in its wake.

Once we had seen a vast flock, an air force of boobies
Commanded, it seemed, by a lone white gull.

We had seen them break from the water, attack
A whole cruise liner of Americans, cheered on by flying fish
As the decks were bespattered and beshat,
The bright shirts ripped and stripped,
Stippled with the blood of Dakota.

It was revenge, of course, for the music and the flashing,
The awful voices and the thud of engines in good fishing time
But it was good to see the boobies bite the complacency
Off the imperial backsides out to sea.

We had even seen the water in the harbour boil, then drain
Suddenly as if the plug of hell had been pulled in a pissing rage
By Satan quenching the fire of his slovenly devils.

Then we ran as he and they cooled down, as he let off steam
And the water, superhot, rushed to swamp the houses and
Place a banana boat in the aisle of the Cathedral, parked so neatly
That Rita nearly gave it a ticket.

We had seen things go wrong and right, even occasional weddings
Before the children were born and called
Industrial non-biblical names,
But we had never seen - not even when the water
Was as crowded as a London tube at five on a Wednesday afternoon
Like a Jamaican election party - we
Had never seen the dolphins
Crash.

III

Along the wharf the schoolgirls, nearlywomen girls
Ranged, their convent skirts bluer than the harbour water,
Flapping as pointlessly, a sea of cloth concealing
Everything but the contours of the bottom.

In the crumpled streets without pavements
Crisp uniforms were everywhere,
Shifts of pink and navy nurses leaking downhill from the hospital,
Each medalled with a watch - the only record
Of island time except the baton
Beating the police band into shape behind sun-crumbled walls
And official pick-up trucks (no questions, no answers).

Where is there to hide in this ragged town
When every wall supports a lazy spy,
A business relationship, a whatever service now,
Where we all watch and play?

Every pillar of the community stops
A house of repute and ill-consideration
Slipping from the hillside
On the ash of the snoozing volcano.

IV

Can an age be right to discover, to unwrap,
Drift, to live unsupported on the slide of a mountain?

Is there an age to braid your hair with glass and gold,
Swim with the fish brushing tight fins against receptive skin
Without the let and hindrance of bashful cloth?

Can the age be right for a mother to be mistaken for a schoolgirl
Or the rampant man for an old sage,
Treasuring his sucked thoughts like a sperm whale
Hoarding air a hundred feet below the pressure of safety?

Can the age be right for loving and leaving behind?

V

The most comforting sight from an island is not the ship
With sails full and ropes thwacking against the mast
In the offshore wind dragged to sea by the sunset.

Neither do the waves flattened
To a rhythm no more troubled than breathing,
Or breezes out of the hurricane months
Carry more than cursory touches of relief.

The sight that slips hope into the soul and excites the
                                                    dormant heart
Is another island, seen clearly in the morning for the first time.

From this littered shore it seems paradise,
Smaller with gentle green peaks, the turquoise of coral rich water,
Maybe a hint of an unexplored interior full of waterfalls
And humming birds and a skiff ready to transport me,
And is that - below the shallow channel - the line
Of a forgotten causeway,
Fordable only on days of auspicion?

VI

Aeneas Arrives at Mount Erycz

Is the fire on the headland more propitious than
The pyre on the continental beach we had deserted?

Looking back across the sea
There was the smoke of the dead against the sunset.

Looking forwards into the dark mountain of the island
The red glow of the holy beacon lit for love (the sailors said),
Though whether for the future or in commemoration
I could not tell then or since in the wandering years.

There was a storm of welcome
That night when we anchored, a viciousness and tenacity
In the bite of the wind on our backs
That would never let us turn, whatever the answer.

Repairs were a week's work.

I was tired of leadership, of the price of decision,
The scorn of indecision, so in the morning
I left the chandlers to their nails, commandeered
Two slaves, females not above fifteen,
Packed food, rolled cloaks
And set a road for the mountain.

There would be a night on her slopes
Whether or not we achieved the summit together.

I expected an arduous climb but easily found the path,
Well trodden, marked by the detritus of lazy pilgrims.

Still it would take all day and I
Was soon too far-gone for marching.

The girls joined hands around my waist,
Buttressed my arms and we meandered to heaven.

Was I ready for Aphrodite?

Her priestesses seemed ready for me, if unimpressed
By my sheepish arrival, the gauche servitude of my companions.

I was tolerated a night's lodging and told to return
When I had more to offer the goddess than guilt
At squandered love and the loyalty of slaves.

VII

I have circled myself with a sea of noise and anonymity,
The cliffs of my chair fortress against conversation.

Age is on my side rendering me as invisible to the firm young
                                                    wayfarers,
Especially the cadet women, as a sandbank in the morning fog,

A November morning fog of unassailable stillness,
The sort that breeds disdain, caresses alienation.

I have the mass of a small continent but bottles,
Comments and salutations pass unobstructed from coast to coast.

I am forgotten geography,
Only spotted on the map at closing time.

VIII

The sad insistence of the waves
Lapping against stone foundations,
Ruffling weed to its perpetual annoyance,
Gave a solemn lilt to the ballad
Of how the island was spoiled.

There was no need for a volcano
To send earth to heaven or turn
Rain to powdered rock, no need
For such a monumental fountain.

Signals were not hard to spot
Though many daily irritations
Were invested with false significance

The noise from engines, for instance
Or the sludge that sat and stank
Along the river banks and infested bridges.

These came after the spoiling
Like the slow demise of flowers
From poison in the water,
No, each rebuttal was born a spoiler

And though they seemed easy enough to sweep away,
For years they bred and colonised with crimson
Field after field of pale green hope
Until the island's reflection in the morning
Sky was livid with their triumph.

IX

Blow the bridges, all of them,
Left to right, bank to bank,
Royalty to university, church to commerce,
Theatre to bookshop. Three of us
Have colonised this point of the tributary island,
Poet, painter, poet, no talking yet,
(We would hate each other's art)
Think, watch the light, the roofs,
The passing dullards of every nation,
So blow the bridges.

Here goes.

X

All islands are linked by the sea, Poseidon's net,
His rape of twisted water. Is it really spume or the
Great god's sperm that spots and crusts
The drying sand?

Within mountains you can trace
That ancient ejaculation
On the knickers of the land.
Will the seed respond
When we expire
Break open with birth delight?

Perhaps he will haul
A mate for my island
Through your Bosphorus
Emancipate the Blest Aegean.

Invocation

Seeking answers has led me nowhere all morning,
The petering lanes as haphazard as the gusting of the wind,
Brambles snagging the mind,
Rare ideas no sooner articulated than
Dropped into the ditch mud.

But flocks of questions fly deftly through the trees,
Laughing, flicking forked tails in disdain.
They are simple enough, part curiosity,
Part exasperated prayer, lines of identification
Scrawled on their shining flanks in garish profusion.

When did the clouds about Olympus turn to concrete?
Why is only one heaven open these days?
What good are altars without sacrifice,
Hymns without libation?
If all the virgins are reserved for martyrs
Who will breed new fools to die for a cause?
Can I opt out, offer other invocations?

Why cannot mortals become stars, merely celebrities,
Now that galaxies have replaced constellations?
When did nymphs become nuns and satyrs apologetic,
Neglecting Apollo, deserting Aphrodite?

Did we drive them to it?
Did you shrug us off as our wars became too nasty
                                        to be good sport,
Deciding that the destitution of our ignorance
                            was small price for Elysium?

Why did you all retire, leaving men to fight alone
Craving the fictional attention of a despotic bully
With three religions all his own,
Each riven by disputatious cults that
Poseidon would never have let compete?

What invocation will lure you back?

Later

All that was left
Was slate grey
In the morning
Tingeing eyes
With the underside of cloud.
Anger subsided with the thunder
The dinge of streets
Exhausted by hot air

Resentful, the sky
Retained a sullen right
To spoil the summer
Unleash another charge.

Nothing happened
Eyes turned green
Old calm
Brought a familiar
Unconsidered smile
A touch
And then the sun.

Fifth Sense

A glance of perfume
Took you to Milan
By blonde hair,
All those rings,
A henge of stones across taut fingers,
A vocal rasp,
Sambucco with the liquorice.

On the blanched olive of your skin
There is no shard of scent,
No memory
Of yesterday or remnant of the night.

Until you reach for a bottle,
Its clear juices
Squeezed from figs,
That fecund fruit,
And fix the moment
For me, the street, the bench,
The grace of your neck at noon.

My Independence Day

My flag has a dozen planets,
Rings intertwined in a confusion of collided moons;
Its predominant colour is black but rimmed with silver,
The severity offset by a golden lion
Who lounges
In the corner, bottom right,
Licking his paws, too tired to bother with a mauling.
All my days are feast days and so it hangs
At half-mast in memory, accusing tribute,
Of all the girls who refused
To revel with me, of all the boys who died
Defending other flags, less amiable,
More demanding. Flags with silly stripes,
Brash primary colours,
On separate poles stuck in desiccated earth,
Trumpets to rouse the hungover before slaughter,
Flags promising the fiction of independence,
Their cloth endowed with injunctions
Against burning, a disrespectful rip.
My flag intertwines the planets with consummate braid.

Gently, of course

Gently, of course, is ideal
But often, how often
The rope, the shoe, the hand, the mouth
Slips
That crucial distance just before the ground.

The expected earth is tarmac,
The bed of feathers a gorse bush, words of comfort
Arrows that find the most vulnerable
To pierce and lodge, barbs forbidding retraction.

Nothing is ever enough
Or timed to matter less,
Money, love nor favour,
Only the letting down is without fail.

The End of the Exhibition

The morning after the masque at court
Ordered by the first Charles Stewart
To blaze the winter far away for one long night,
A traveller from Scotland, recusant,
Was so shattered by the transformation, light to dirt,
He renounced the world, turned monast.

So this room, denied these colours, will seem bereft,
A shadow space, its form unkempt,
The conversation that these pictures brought
Long ceased, mid-sentence, cut short.
In their reassembly, new but separate,
Their lasting fight will be to startle all that's left.

Aspects of Sea

I

Beside

Fresh as sand castle
Friends met this morning as the moat was dug
And reinforced with pebble ramparts we ran free at last,
Never asked why we rampaged
From the tide-line to wave edge and back,
Our yelps and admonitions drowned in the rasp of shingle
The piled debris of a conflict the land always lost.

We could be as careless as the surf of breakages,
Breaking ages, voices raised
In shrill tones as random as thunder.

We children were too busy to stare patiently across the water
Waiting for an incident at the horizon,
A three shift in green from turquoise via olive to forest
A sudden shock of grey - too excited
To mind the swift drench of a shower from an unexpected quarter
A cold rush before the golden sun took charge once more.

There's so much, so much to be done before the tide wins;
Brothers to be buried in hummocks of sand
Ice cream to make drops so sisters cry
Crabs to chase until the years collect
And turn us into lovers too enthralled to turn back along the beach.

II

Under

There is no such thing as darkness.

Here only humans with their pathetic little eyes and
                                          fragile ears
Are sightless unless near the burning glare
The poisoned air untempered by healing water.

Sailing free of weight and wind the speed
Is always cruising whether dive or rise
Gulf stream warm or Antarctic chilled.

We glide round mountains
Navigate chasms without stars
Never need a cable or space spy to talk long distance.

We love to watch you sink
Laugh as you paddle home and thank you for giving us
So many ships to decorate with flowers in our
                                 garden toy collection.

III

On

On deck fear is loud
Never heard, force ten is louder,
Surround sound
Illegal power
Anarchic dissonance
No plan, no negotiation
With air propelled beyond fury
Water that sucks, spits,
Shoves like a rapist high on destruction
Loving the feel of the ship's disintegration
Strewing debris in exultation
Some to be worn on waves' crests
Some sent as trophies below
To be encrusted
Fondled on the seabed.

Prayer is drowned before the pray-er.

Shatter the amen, buckle ship's buttress,
Flood and reflood
Send its nave to howling heaven
Render vestments rags.

For the fun of it,
The sheer spume-shot laughter
Let them live
These jellied men and salt-soaked women
Let morning bring calm and silent recrimination
Deliverance without trust.

IV

Above

White horses dance in the unexpected sun to spread the gold,
Flicking their manes in the wind that set them free to run all night,
Only spotted by the lights of an indifferent trawler
But they and their gale are soon
Exhausted in this golden dawn,
The taming sun whispers them to deep stable,

Closing a door of brilliant glass, and conjures haze
That joins air and water, uneasy twins told to kiss
And make up in public view.

Leave them to their surliness slowly, without giving offence,
Though they'll never notice; rise from them, fly up
As though backing away from a king.

Sea king now, filling the vision even as distance increases,
Great islands reduced to pimples on the water's majesty
That erupt, outstay their welcome and submerge forgotten.

Breaking free of the sea king's gaze, rising through his myopia,
The divisions in his kingdom emerge, untidy,
Jagged, the pathology of earth.

Why call it Earth when so much is the Sea?
Why call us man when so many more
Are women and we are mostly water too?

Soon the sea can no longer hide his curves
But there his humility ends
For, as the feet become thousands and the miles mimic them,
Though the sky gathers its clouds to shroud him,
The majesty, the royal blue of his coat,
Enthrals the planets in the name of peace.

Acknowledgements

Acknowledgements are due to the editors of the following publications where some of these poems were first published: 'An Incident of War' first appeared in *The Liberal*, as did 'A Vote for Absence'. 'Translated Daughter' and 'A Prayer for a New Goddaughter' were published by *Poetry Wales*. 'Above' (IV of Aspects of Sea) was in *Orbis*.

'Presteigne Festival/Gwaithla 25 Years On' was commissioned for the 2007 Presteigne Festival. The first of the Radnor Songs, 'The Buzzard', was commissioned for the 2004 Presteigne Festival, set by Cecilia McDowall and recorded as part of *A Garland for Presteigne* by soprano Gillian Keith and pianist Simon Lepper on the Metronome label. The full cycle was set by Cecilia McDowall and performed by Rachel Nichols and Paul Plummer for the 2005 festival. The orchestral version, with Orchestra Nova conducted by George Vass, was given its first London performance in St. John's Smith Square on 9 October 2011 and is available on Dutton Epoch records and from Oxford University Press. Cecilia also asked for 'Aspects of Sea' to be written as text for a proposed sea symphony.

'The New Senedd, Cardiff' was commissioned for it's opening by Academi Cymreig/The Welsh Academy. 'My Independence Day' was written for the 2005 Bay Lit Festival, Cardiff. 'Citrus' was published in English and Serbian as part of the 11 9/Web Streaming Poetry anthology by Auropolis, Belgrade. 'Deceptive Beauty' (IV of 'More for Helen of Troy') was ordered by the designer Ewgeniya Lyras who illustrates it in the cover photograph.